W9-BXK-943

American Moments

ABDO
Daughters

RECONSTRUCTION

By Alan Pierce

VISIT US AT
WWW.ABDOPUB.COM

Published by ABDO Publishing Company, 4940 Viking Drive, Suite 622, Edina, Minnesota 55435. Copyright © 2005 by Abdo Consulting Group, Inc. International copyrights reserved in all countries. No part of this book may be reproduced in any form without written permission from the publisher. ABDO & Daughters™ is a trademark and logo of ABDO Publishing Company.

Printed in the United States.

Edited by: Melanie A. Howard
Interior Production and Design: Terry Dunham Incorporated
Cover Design: Mighty Media
Photos: Corbis, Library of Congress, North Wind Pictures

Library of Congress Cataloging-in-Publication Data

Pierce, Alan, 1966-
    Reconstruction / Alan Pierce.
        p. cm. -- (American moments)
    Includes index.
    ISBN 1-59197-939-0
    1. Reconstruction (U.S. history, 1865-1877)--Juvenile literature. I. Title. II. Series.

E668.P535 2005
973.8--dc22
                                                              2004062702

CONTENTS

JUBILEE OF FREEDOM

In late March 1865, thousands of people watched an astonishing event in Charleston, South Carolina. African Americans had organized a parade to celebrate their recent deliverance from slavery. More than 4,000 men, women, and children marched through the city's streets. As slaves they had served masters and were considered property. Now they were free. One banner in the parade expressed the joy of the African Americans. It read, "We know no masters but ourselves."

One scene in the parade demonstrated the cruelty of slavery. A man pretended to sell two women at an auction. The sight prompted an emotional response from some of the women in the crowd. They shouted, "Give me back my children!" During slavery, members of slave families had been sold at auctions. Sometimes slave families were broken up in these sales.

Another scene in the parade signaled the end of slavery. African Americans carried a coffin with the words "Slavery is Dead" written on the side. This sight caused people in the crowd to celebrate. One newspaper article described the parade as a "jubilee of freedom." The word *jubilee* is a biblical term that refers to a time when slaves were set free.

African Americans celebrate as the Union army marches through Charleston, South Carolina.

The parade could take place because the government that supported slavery was losing power in South Carolina. South Carolina and ten other states had voted to leave the United States between 1860 and 1861. These states formed the Confederate States of America. The Northern states and a few slave states remained loyal to the federal government in Washington DC. These states were known as the Union. The Union invaded the rebellious Southern states in order to preserve the country. The conflict between the Union and the Confederacy was known as the Civil War.

During the Civil War, the Union army helped liberate about 4 million slaves. The end of slavery raised many difficult questions. Americans argued about what rights should be granted to the recently freed slaves. Northern leaders also struggled with the question of restoring Southern states to the Union. These questions were debated in a process called Reconstruction.

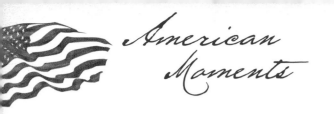

THE ROAD TO WAR

Americans had quarreled about slavery for decades. Slavery was more common in Southern states. Many landowners there relied on slavery to plant and harvest cotton. This crop required a long growing season that existed in Southern states. But in Northern states the demand for slaves was far less. In the late eighteenth and early nineteenth centuries, Northern states took steps to abolish slavery.

For many people, slavery was a moral issue. Christian groups, such as the Quakers, believed that slavery was a sin. The Quakers and other Christians believed that all people were equal before God. Slavery ruined this relationship of equality.

Many Americans also believed that slavery violated the nation's principles. The country had been founded on the ideas of equality and liberty. In 1776, Thomas Jefferson had written in the Declaration of Independence that "We hold these truths to be self-evident, that all men are created equal . . . " Some Americans assumed that Jefferson meant that all white men were born equal. Others disagreed. They claimed that there was a conflict between slavery and claims of equality.

In 1854, an event provoked more tension between supporters and opponents of slavery. Congress passed the Kansas-Nebraska Act.

Thomas Jefferson

This legislation allowed people in the territories of Kansas and Nebraska to decide whether to permit slavery. Northerners were outraged. An earlier agreement had prohibited slavery in this area. But the Kansas-Nebraska Act made it possible for slavery to spread into areas where it had been banned.

The Kansas-Nebraska Act motivated the opponents of slavery to form a new political party. In 1854, antislavery supporters held political conventions in Ripon, Wisconsin, and Jackson, Michigan. These conventions led to a new political party called the Republican Party. The Republicans urged Congress to abolish slavery in U.S. territories.

Abraham Lincoln was one of those who despised the Kansas-Nebraska Act. He believed that slavery was evil, and he strongly opposed its expansion. Lincoln had served in the Illinois legislature and U.S. Congress as a member of the Whig Party. However, the Whig Party was divided between opponents and supporters of slavery. Lincoln searched for a new political party to join. In 1856, he became a member of the Republican Party.

Lincoln quickly established himself as a Republican leader. In 1858, he ran in Illinois for a seat in the U.S. Senate. His opponent from the Democratic Party was Senator Stephen A. Douglas. Douglas had proposed the Kansas-Nebraska Act while serving in the Senate.

Abraham Lincoln

Stephen A. Douglas

The two candidates held a series of debates around Illinois. The debates gave Lincoln and Douglas a chance to express their views about slavery. In the first debate, Lincoln referred to the Declaration of Independence. The declaration listed a series of rights, including the right to life, liberty, and the pursuit of happiness. Lincoln insisted that blacks were entitled to these rights.

Although Lincoln lost the election, the debates made Lincoln well-known in the Republican Party. Many people encouraged Lincoln to run for president. In 1860, Lincoln ran for president as the Republican candidate. His candidacy alarmed whites in Southern states. Lincoln promised not to overturn slavery in the South. But Southerners believed Lincoln would weaken slavery if he won the presidency.

Lincoln entered the 1860 presidential election in a strong position. After he won the nomination, Lincoln ran with the backing of a unified Republican Party. Meanwhile, the Democratic Party had fallen into confusion. Delegates at the Democratic convention nominated Douglas as the party's presidential candidate. However, Southern Democrats were unhappy with Douglas. They nominated their own candidate, John C. Breckinridge. He was serving as U.S. vice president at the time.

Another political party offered John Bell as a presidential candidate. Bell was a former U.S. senator from Tennessee. He ran as a candidate for the Constitutional Union Party. This party tried to give less attention to slavery. Instead, the party emphasized loyalty to the Constitution and the Union. Bell was chosen to be the party's candidate because he supported both the Union and slavery.

In the election, voters in the South split their votes among Breckinridge, Bell, and Douglas. Lincoln won all the Northern states except for part of New Jersey. By winning the North, Lincoln won the presidency.

Lincoln's election triggered a crisis. In December, South Carolina held a convention to consider an ordinance of secession. The ordinance was the process by which South Carolina officially broke away from the Union. On December 20, delegates passed the ordinance 169–0. Within the next few weeks, Alabama, Florida, Georgia, Louisiana, Mississippi, and Texas seceded.

Southern forces began capturing U.S. forts and arsenals in states that had left the Union. Major Robert Anderson commanded the federal stronghold of Fort Sumter in Charleston Harbor, South Carolina. He refused to surrender the fort. On April 12, 1861, Southern cannons fired upon Fort Sumter. Anderson surrendered the fort 30 hours later. The fighting at Fort Sumter signaled the start of the Civil War.

Robert Anderson

TOTAL WAR

After Southerners captured Fort Sumter, Lincoln asked loyal states to provide 75,000 troops to fight the rebellion. Lincoln's request forced the states to decide whether to fight the rebellion or join it. Arkansas, North Carolina, Tennessee, and Virginia decided to secede. These four states and the seven states that had already seceded formed the Confederate States of America. In July 1861, the Confederacy located its capital in Richmond, Virginia.

Not all the slave states seceded. Delaware, Kentucky, Maryland, and Missouri remained in the Union. These four states were commonly referred to as the Border States. In order to assure their loyalty, Lincoln emphasized that the war was being fought to preserve the Union. An announcement that the war was being waged to end slavery might offend these states, and cause their secession.

Lincoln expected a quick war. He expected soldiers to serve about 90 days. The war, however, did not end quickly. In July 1861, Union troops commanded by General Irvin McDowell marched toward Richmond. McDowell's army attacked Confederate forces near Bull Run creek. However, the Confederate soldiers repelled the Union army and sent the Northern soldiers retreating in confusion. The First Battle of Bull Run ended in a Confederate victory.

Union generals then adopted a policy of total war to defeat the Confederacy. Total war meant the North would use its advantages to

CREATION OF WEST VIRGINIA

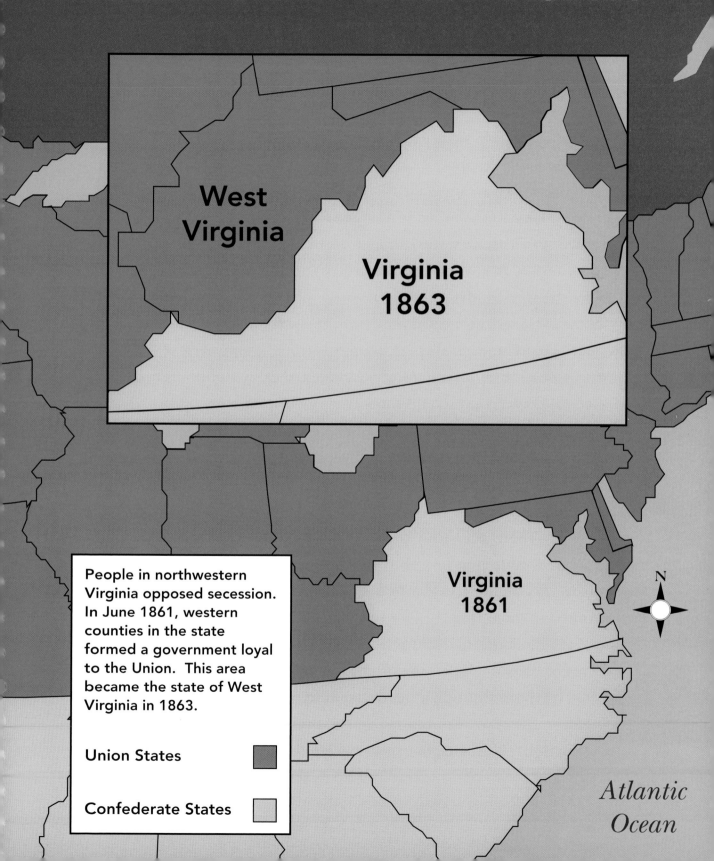

West Virginia

Virginia 1863

Virginia 1861

People in northwestern Virginia opposed secession. In June 1861, western counties in the state formed a government loyal to the Union. This area became the state of West Virginia in 1863.

Union States

Confederate States

N

Atlantic Ocean

crush the South. These advantages included a larger population, and therefore an ability to field bigger armies. The North had about 22 million people compared to the South's 9 million people. Slaves accounted for about 3.5 million of the South's population. Northern states also had more factories than Southern states. This meant the Union could better equip its armies.

Despite its advantages, the North did poorly at the beginning of the war. Many Republicans in Congress were upset by the lack of progress. In December 1861, they formed the Joint Committee on the Conduct of the War. This committee pressed for replacing General George B. McClellan, who was head of the Union army.

Some of those who created the committee were known as Radical Republicans. These members of Congress strongly supported emancipation for the slaves. Moreover, the Radical Republicans believed the federal government should support emancipation more openly. They also favored deploying black troops to fight the Confederacy.

The struggle between Union and Confederate forces led to a staggering amount of deaths in battle. On September 17, 1862, Union and Confederate forces fought near Antietam Creek in western Maryland. The Union army prevented the Confederates from possibly capturing Washington DC. But the cost of lives was enormous. The Confederate army lost well over 13,000 men, while Union deaths amounted to more than 12,000 soldiers. The Battle of Antietam was one of the bloodiest days of the war.

This battle was also an important victory for the Union. President Lincoln used the triumph as an occasion to address slavery. On September 22, 1862, Lincoln issued the preliminary Emancipation Proclamation. This announcement declared that all slaves held in

Lincoln and his cabinet discuss the Emancipation Proclamation.

rebel states would be freed. To avoid this, these states would have to return to the Union by January 1, 1863. No states accepted Lincoln's offer to return to the Union by that date. On January 1, Lincoln issued the Emancipation Proclamation.

In reality, the Emancipation Proclamation did little to free slaves. The proclamation affected areas beyond the control of Union armies. Slaves in the loyal states of Delaware, Kentucky, Maryland, and Missouri were not freed by the proclamation. The proclamation also did not free slaves in Confederate territory conquered by the North. These areas included Tennessee, southern Louisiana, and some of Virginia. However, the proclamation expanded the purpose of the Civil War. The North was fighting for the slaves' freedom as well as the Union's preservation.

Some leaders in the Republican Party believed stronger action was needed against slavery. The Emancipation Proclamation was a wartime order. Many feared the Emancipation Proclamation would not be legal after the war. Republicans urged Lincoln to support a constitutional amendment to abolish slavery. Lincoln began to devote more political support for an amendment to end slavery for good.

LINCOLN AND THE RADICALS

Throughout 1863, Union forces failed to capture Richmond. But Northern troops had more success along the Mississippi River. In July, forces led by Union general Ulysses S. Grant captured the city of Vicksburg, Mississippi. This victory, and another Union win in Louisiana, gave the North control of the Mississippi River.

By late 1863, Union forces controlled the Confederate states of Louisiana, Arkansas, and Tennessee. On December 8, Lincoln announced his plan for restoring Confederate states to the Union. It was called the Proclamation of Amnesty and Reconstruction.

The plan was merciful toward the Confederates. His proposal called for Southerners to swear a loyalty oath to the United States. Not many Southerners had to take the oath before their states were restored to the Union. Once 10 percent of the voters who cast ballots in 1860 swore oaths, these states could form new governments. For this reason, Lincoln's proposal was sometimes called the Ten Percent Plan.

Lincoln's plan also required Southerners to abolish slavery. After ending slavery and taking the oath, most Southerners would have their rights restored. Only high-ranking Confederate leaders would be excluded from this amnesty.

During the war, governments loyal to the Union were established in Arkansas, Louisiana, Tennessee, and Virginia. Lincoln believed these governments met the conditions of his plan. However, Congress did not acknowledge these state governments.

The Radical Republicans opposed Lincoln's Ten Percent Plan. They believed that Lincoln was far too easy on the Confederates. The Radicals were also disappointed that Lincoln had not devoted more attention to the slaves. They believed that freed slaves should be guaranteed the right to vote.

Two members of the Radical Republicans proposed a different policy. Representative Henry W. Davis of Maryland and Senator Benjamin F. Wade of Ohio sponsored the Wade-Davis Bill. Their plan for Reconstruction was tougher on the South than Lincoln's policy. A majority of white men in the Confederate states would have to take an oath of allegiance to the United States. These states would also have to adopt constitutions acceptable to Congress and the president. After these requirements were met, these states could return to the Union.

The bill did not discuss

Benjamin F. Wade

voting rights for blacks. Most Republicans did not support this idea. But the bill directed Southern states to give blacks equal treatment before the law.

Congress passed the bill on July 2, 1864. Lincoln, however, did not sign it into law. The president's veto angered Radical Republicans. The fight over the bill signaled a fierce battle about Reconstruction.

In March 1864, Lincoln had appointed Grant as commander of all the Union armies. Grant outlined a strategy that called for his army to engage the forces of Confederate general Robert E. Lee in northern Virginia. Meanwhile, Union general William T. Sherman would attack Confederate general Joseph E. Johnston's army in northern Georgia.

In April, Grant wrote to Sherman, "You I propose to move against Johnston's army, to break it up, and to get into the interior of the enemy's country as far as you can, inflicting all the damage you can against their war resources."

William T. Sherman

Sherman's army sets fires and destroys railroad tracks in Atlanta, Georgia.

Sherman launched his attack in May. Johnston avoided a major battle with Sherman's stronger army. Confederate president Jefferson Davis replaced Johnston with General John Bell Hood. Hood's forces attacked Sherman's army, but the Confederates lost. In September, Sherman's troops captured Atlanta, Georgia, and burned the city to the ground.

The Union army's capture of Atlanta was good news for President Lincoln. In 1864, he was running for reelection against former Union general George B. McClellan. Lincoln needed a military triumph to show that the North was making progress in the war. Sherman's conquest of Atlanta helped provide Lincoln with that victory.

The Republicans named Andrew Johnson as Lincoln's running mate and vice presidential candidate. Johnson had not even been a Republican. Instead, he had been a Democratic U.S. senator from Tennessee. He had also owned slaves before the war. But when Southern states began to secede, he was faithful to the Union. Republicans nominated Johnson for vice president because they hoped he would appeal to Democratic voters. In November, Lincoln and Johnson won the election.

That same month, Sherman led an army of about 60,000 soldiers through Georgia. He aimed to carry out Grant's orders of inflicting all the damage he could. The army moved in two columns and cut a swath of destruction more than 50 miles (80 km) wide.

Sherman's troops lived off supplies they found. They seized livestock and vegetables from farms. Union soldiers burned down homes and other buildings. Georgians referred to the smoldering remains of chimneys as "Sherman's Sentinels." Troops also destroyed the railroad system by tearing up tracks.

This campaign became known as Sherman's March to the Sea. Sherman said he intended to "make Georgia howl." He wanted Georgians to experience the hardships of war. But there was a strategic reason for the destruction. The Union troops were destroying materials that could be used to supply Confederate armies. Sherman also hoped Confederate soldiers would desert from the army to protect their homes.

On December 21, 1864, Sherman's March to the Sea ended when Union troops captured Savannah, Georgia. General Sherman telegraphed Lincoln with the message, "I beg to present you, as a Christmas gift, the city of Savannah."

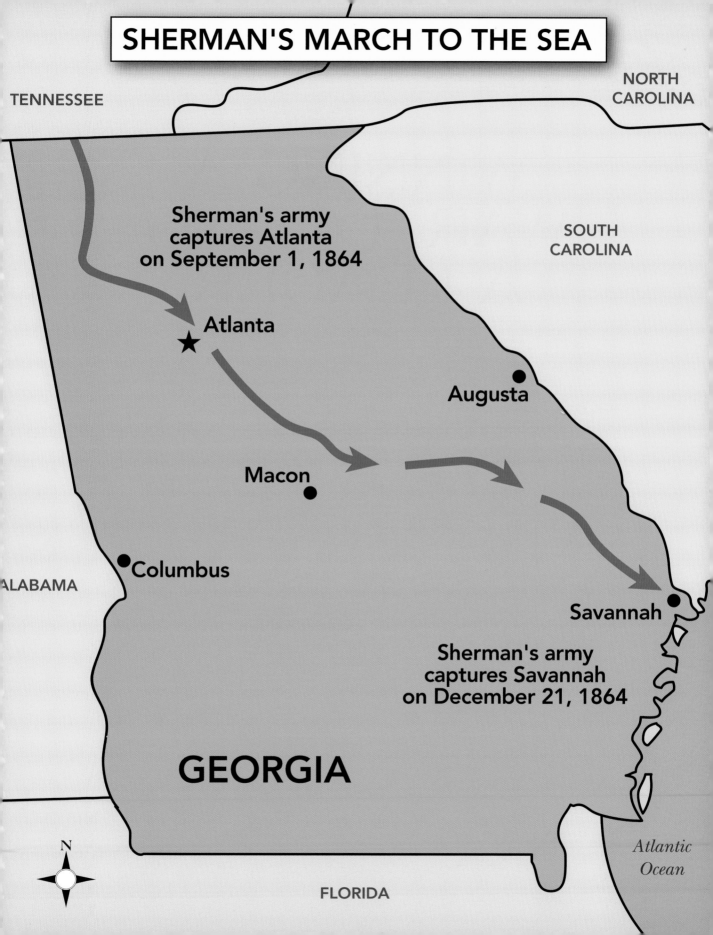

SHERMAN'S MARCH TO THE SEA

TENNESSEE

NORTH CAROLINA

Sherman's army captures Atlanta on September 1, 1864

★ Atlanta

SOUTH CAROLINA

Augusta

Macon

ALABAMA

Columbus

Savannah

Sherman's army captures Savannah on December 21, 1864

GEORGIA

N

Atlantic Ocean

FLORIDA

WINNING A WAR, LOSING A LEADER

In early 1865, the military situation was favorable for the Union. Grant's army had pinned down Lee's forces around Richmond. Sherman's army invaded South Carolina in January. As the Confederacy collapsed, the North took more steps to abolish slavery.

The U.S. Senate had already passed the Thirteenth Amendment. On January 31, 1865, the U.S. House of Representatives finally approved it. To become part of the Constitution, the amendment needed to be ratified by 27 states. By late February, 19 legislatures had ratified the amendment.

Meanwhile, the federal government took action to help the 4 million freed slaves. On March 3, 1865, Congress established the Bureau of Refugees, Freedmen, and Abandoned Lands. The agency is better known as the Freedmen's Bureau. It was supposed to exist for one year.

The bureau was set up to provide food, clothing, and health care to the freed slaves. In addition, the bureau was responsible for providing former slaves with an education. Most slaves were not prepared for life in the war-torn South. Educating slaves was strongly discouraged in the South. In some states it was illegal.

John Wilkes Booth assassinates President Lincoln at Ford's Theatre.

In the spring, the war drew to an end. Lee's army abandoned Richmond on the night of April 2. With his army badly outnumbered and hungry, Lee decided to quit fighting. On April 9, he surrendered to Grant near Appomattox Court House.

At this time, the Union suffered a terrible blow to its leadership. On the night of April 14, Lincoln attended a play at Ford's Theatre in Washington DC. During the performance, a man named John Wilkes Booth shot the president in the head. Booth was a fierce supporter of the Confederacy. He broke a leg while fleeing, but managed to escape. Lincoln was taken to a nearby lodging house where he died in the morning.

On April 26, soldiers trapped Booth in a shed in northeast Virginia. Booth died from a gunshot. No one knows if he shot himself or was killed by a soldier.

THE FIGHT OVER RECONSTRUCTION

The death of Lincoln elevated Johnson to the presidency. Johnson faced a difficult task. The war had taken a frightening toll on the entire nation. More than 600,000 Union and Confederate troops had died in the war. Thousands of other men had been wounded. Sherman's campaign had slashed a path of destruction through Georgia. Large areas of Mississippi had been devastated. Union troops had also destroyed Charleston and Columbia in South Carolina. Richmond was in ruins.

Reconstruction was also Johnson's problem. At first, Johnson and the Radical Republicans seemed to share common views. In 1864, Johnson had talked about punishing Confederate leaders. He also seemed interested in the condition of the slaves. In one speech, he promised to lead blacks toward a future of liberty and peace.

Although Johnson believed in freedom for the slaves, he did not accept political equality for blacks. Moreover, Johnson did not want equality for freed slaves to interfere with readmitting the former Confederate states. Whites should continue to control the South, Johnson believed.

In May 1865, Johnson recognized the state governments in Arkansas, Louisiana, Tennessee, and Virginia. These states had formed governments under Lincoln's plan. But none of these states allowed blacks to vote.

Andrew Johnson

Hyla Library

On May 29, 1865, President Johnson revealed his plan for Reconstruction. The plan called for pardoning most people who had rebelled against the Union. They would have all their property restored to them except for slaves. In exchange, they would have to swear an oath of loyalty to the United States. High-ranking former Confederates and large property owners could apply to the president for amnesty.

Johnson's plan also called for the former Confederate states to hold state conventions. These conventions had several aims. Delegates were to consider repealing the ordinances of secession, canceling Confederate war debt, and ratifying the Thirteenth Amendment. Once these obligations were met, these states would be admitted to the Union.

President Johnson's proposals did not deal with whether the freed slaves should vote. He thought this issue should be left up to the states. This viewpoint fit with Johnson's belief that states should decide many issues for themselves.

The former Confederate states were not expanding rights for former slaves. In fact, the new state governments in the South were limiting freedom for blacks. By late 1865, Mississippi and South Carolina had passed laws called Black Codes. Other former Confederate states also adopted these laws. These codes were intended to maintain white control over African Americans. They barred African Americans from having guns, voting, or serving on juries.

Black Codes were also tough on vagrancy. African Americans were forced to prove they had jobs. If they could not prove they had employment, they could be jailed and fined. African Americans who could not pay fines would be hired out to employers.

White voters in South Carolina line up to take an oath of loyalty to the Union.

African Americans were even more outraged by apprenticeship laws. These laws allowed white employers to use African-American orphans for unpaid labor. The laws also affected African-American parents who were deemed unable to support their children. Judges had the power to take these children away and turn them over to white employers. The Freedmen's Bureau received many appeals for help from African-American parents whose children had been taken away.

Apprenticeship laws reminded African Americans of the tragedy of slavery. Slave families were frequently torn apart when family members were sold off by masters. Slavery had been abolished, but African-American families were being separated again.

At this time, African Americans experienced one victory. On December 6, 1865, Georgia became the twenty-seventh state to ratify the Thirteenth Amendment. The amendment abolishing slavery then became part of the U.S. Constitution.

PRESIDENT V. CONGRESS

The Radical Republicans were troubled about the way Reconstruction was going. They were offended by the Black Codes. Another development also angered them. In December 1865, the congressional delegations from the Confederate states arrived in Washington DC to take their seats. Many of these legislators had been important Confederate officers and leaders. For example, the newly elected U.S. senator from Georgia was Alexander Stephens. He had served as vice president of the Confederacy.

Republicans prevented the Southern legislators from assuming seats in Congress. They did this by telling clerks in the House and the Senate to bypass Southern legislators when the roll of congressional members was called. By doing this, Republicans rejected the Southern state government established under Johnson's leadership.

Congress began to set up its own policies for Reconstruction. In February 1866, Congress voted to continue the Freedmen's Bureau. According to Congress's plan, the bureau would have more power. The bureau would have the authority to help African Americans in legal cases. In the South, African Americans were not receiving justice in the courts.

In March, Congress passed the Civil Rights Act of 1866. This bill would grant American citizenship to most people born in the United

CARPETBAGGERS

An illustration of a carpetbagger traveling from Wisconsin to Missouri

During Reconstruction, several Northerners traveled to the South to become businessmen and politicians. These Northerners were often called carpetbaggers. Carpetbagger was an unfavorable term. It implied that many Northerners who arrived in the South had few possessions. They were said to fit all their property in a sack known as a carpetbag. These carpetbaggers hoped to use the new group of voting, free blacks for political and financial gain.

Many carpetbaggers were concerned about blacks. However, several carpetbaggers used the newly formed Reconstruction governments to carry out dishonest financial schemes. This helped give Reconstruction governments in the South a reputation for being corrupt.

Southerners who supported Reconstruction were known as scalawags. These Southerners made up 20 percent of the white voting population. They came from all kinds of backgrounds.

The labels scalawag and carpetbagger indicate the unpopularity of Reconstruction supporters in the South. These words are still unkind terms. Today, scalawag indicates a worthless person. Carpetbagger has come to mean an outsider, especially one who interferes with politics.

Blacks line up to receive aid at the Freedmen's Bureau.

States. Only Native Americans were not included in the bill. The bill also guaranteed rights to U.S. citizens regardless of race. These included the rights to enjoy laws that protected the security of people and property.

The conflict between Congress and President Johnson became more hostile. Johnson vetoed the Freedmen's Bureau and the civil rights bills. He believed these bills gave the federal government too much power. Also, Johnson did not think African Americans should be citizens. Congress, however, gathered enough votes to defeat Johnson's veto and pass the bills. For the first time in U.S. history, Congress had overcome a veto to pass a major law.

Despite the victories over the vetoes, Republicans feared a reversal. They were worried that Southerners in Congress might eventually overturn the Civil Rights Act. Radical Republicans began working on a constitutional amendment. The purpose of this amendment was to strengthen rights for African Americans and to combat the Black Codes.

The proposed Fourteenth Amendment contained several clauses, or sections. The first section guaranteed citizenship to all people born in the United States. It also forbade states from restricting the rights of its citizens.

The amendment, however, did not guarantee African-American men the right to vote. But one section threatened to reduce Congressional representation of states that curbed voting rights of black men. Republicans insisted that former Confederate states ratify the amendment before being admitted to the Union.

In June 1866, Congress passed the Fourteenth Amendment. The amendment then went to the states for ratification. Tennessee ratified the amendment in July. This allowed Tennessee to seat its senators and representatives in Congress.

One artist's idea of the nation rebuilding itself during Reconstruction

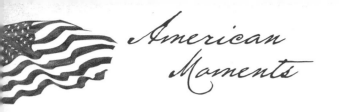

IMPEACHMENT

In 1867, Congress continued to take charge of Reconstruction. On March 2, it passed the Reconstruction Act of 1867. This established military rule of the South. The former Confederacy, except for Tennessee, was divided into five military districts. Each district was ruled by a general who was almost all-powerful. This military rule was backed up by 20,000 federal soldiers stationed in the South.

Congress passed another important law called the Tenure of Office Act on March 2. This act strengthened the power of Congress and weakened the authority of the president. The president appointed many people to political office. Sometimes the consent of the Senate was needed for appointment. The Tenure of Office Act concerned the resignations of officials who had been appointed with Senate approval. The act compelled the president to get permission from the Senate before dismissing these officials.

The Tenure of Office Act provoked a confrontation between Congress and President Johnson in the summer of 1867. Johnson wished to challenge the constitutionality of the act. He also wanted to remove Secretary of War Edwin M. Stanton from office. Johnson and Stanton disagreed about Reconstruction. Stanton tended to agree more with the Republicans in Congress about policies for the South.

Johnson tried to replace Stanton with General Grant. This plan did not work, and Johnson fired Stanton in February 1868.

Edwin M. Stanton

Republicans in Congress then tried to remove the president from office. On February 24, the House of Representatives voted to impeach Johnson. This was the first time in U.S. history that the House had voted to impeach a president.

Impeachment meant that Johnson would face a trial in the U.S. Senate on charges spelled out by the House. Representatives announced 11 charges against Johnson. Most of the charges had to do with Johnson's removal of Stanton. Other charges accused Johnson of dishonoring Congress and failing to enforce Reconstruction laws.

The trial in the Senate began on March 30. Lawyers for Johnson argued that the House of Representatives had failed to accuse the president of committing a crime. On May 16, the Senate voted 35–19 to convict Johnson. However, this total was not enough to remove Johnson from office. One more vote for conviction was needed. The Senate held two more votes in May, but the vote total was the same. Johnson remained president.

The president owed his political survival to some Republican senators. Republicans despised Johnson's Reconstruction policy. But some Republican senators felt the legal case against the president was weak. These senators refused to convict Johnson.

Meanwhile, more states continued to ratify the Fourteenth Amendment. Alabama, Arkansas, Florida, Louisiana, North Carolina, and South Carolina ratified the amendment. This allowed them to be readmitted to the Union. On July 28, 1868, the amendment was added to the Constitution.

Republicans were still concerned about the voting rights of African Americans. The 1868 presidential election showed the importance of African-American votes. In that election, Republican candidate Ulysses S. Grant ran against Democratic candidate Horatio

Seymour. Historians believe that Grant received 500,000 votes from African Americans. These votes helped Grant defeat Seymour.

Congressional Republicans began to work on another constitutional amendment. This amendment was designed to protect the voting rights of African-American men. The amendment prohibited states from restricting voting rights because of race or previous condition of servitude. In February 1869, Congress passed the proposed Fifteenth Amendment. Congress required Georgia, Mississippi, Texas, and Virginia to ratify the amendment before being restored to the Union.

Virginia ratified the Fifteenth Amendment in October 1869. Georgia, Mississippi, and Texas ratified the amendment in the winter of 1870. By March, the Fifteenth Amendment had become part of the Constitution. All the former Confederate states had now been restored to the Union.

A Harper's Weekly *drawing shows Ulysses S. Grant vanquishing Horatio Seymour.*

FREEDOM UNFULFILLED

Reconstruction was making a difference in the South. African Americans were serving in political offices. Some even served in the U.S. Congress. Hiram Revels was the first African-American U.S. senator. In 1870, he was elected to finish the term of Jefferson Davis, who had been Mississippi's senator before the war.

Revels only served from 1870 to 1871. But another African American named Blanche K. Bruce served longer in the Senate. Like Revels, Bruce represented Mississippi. Bruce was elected to the Senate in 1874. He served from 1875 to 1881.

Many more African Americans held state and local political offices. Several hundred African Americans served in state legislatures during Reconstruction. Most of these state legislators had been former slaves. Also, some African Americans served as mayors and sheriffs.

Many whites in the South resented the political power held by African Americans. They also hated the Republican Party. Sometimes this anger took a violent form. After the Civil War, white men in the South formed violent organizations. One of these groups was the Ku Klux Klan.

The Ku Klux Klan targeted African Americans and Republican leaders. The Klan started in Tennessee in 1866. Klan members

This drawing shows the progress African Americans made as a result of Reconstruction. The three largest figures are Blanche K. Bruce (left), *Frederick Douglass* (center) *and Hiram Revels.*

believed in the superiority of white people. They disguised themselves in white robes and hoods.

Members of Congress were outraged by the behavior of the Klan. In April 1871, Congress passed the Ku Klux Klan Act. This act allowed the federal government to use troops against the Klan. The act was successful. Klan activity subsided after the act became law. However, the Klan never entirely went away.

Throughout the late 1860s and early 1870s, Republicans lost power in Southern states. Southerners elected Democratic legislators and governors. These Democratic governments ended Radical Reconstruction in the Southern states.

In 1875, Congress once more attempted to protect the rights of African Americans. Congress passed the Civil Rights Act of 1875. This act prohibited discrimination in public places such as hotels and theaters. However, the law was not strongly enforced.

By 1876, the political situation was changing in the United States. A Republican had served as president since 1860. But Democrats hoped their candidate might win the election in 1876. That year's presidential election featured Republican Rutherford B. Hayes and Democrat Samuel Tilden. Hayes was the former governor of Ohio. Tilden served as governor of New York.

The election turned out to be controversial. Tilden received about 247,000 more popular votes than Hayes. However, the vote total in the electoral college failed to reveal a winner. Confusion arose because Louisiana, Florida, and South Carolina had conflicting vote totals in the electoral college. One vote return was Republican and the other one was Democratic. Both Republicans and Democrats claimed the electoral votes from these states.

A crisis was avoided with the Compromise of 1877. In January, Congress established an electoral commission to count the electoral votes. In February, the commission counted the electoral vote totals. The commission accepted the Republican electoral vote totals, which gave Hayes the victory.

Democrats also issued a demand in return for allowing Hayes to assume the presidency. They wanted federal troops withdrawn from Louisiana and South Carolina. Hayes kept this part of the compromise when he became president. In 1877, federal troops left these two Southern states. The withdrawal marked the end of

Reconstruction. It also signaled the end of Republican efforts to protect the rights of African Americans in the South.

The Republican abandonment of Reconstruction left the South in the hands of the Democrats. This situation was a disaster for African Americans living in the South. Whites began to take away the political power of African Americans. For a few years, African-American men continued to vote. But Southern state legislators put up barriers to this right. For example, they set up a poll tax.

Rutherford B. Hayes

This was a tax people had to pay before they voted. Many African Americans could not afford the tax, so they could not vote.

Southern states also began passing laws to separate the blacks and whites in most situations. Laws separated the races in restaurants, parks, and theaters. Signs saying "White Only" and "Colored Only" appeared over building entrances, drinking fountains, and restrooms. These laws imposed a system known as segregation. This policy was designed to eliminate any social contact between the two races.

Frederick Douglass, a writer and former slave, reflected on the conditions of African Americans. In 1882, he wrote, "Though slavery was abolished, the wrongs of my people were not ended. Though they were not slaves, they were not yet quite free."

Douglass's comment pointed out that Reconstruction had failed in some ways and succeeded in others. Slavery had ended. Congress had worked to protect the rights of African Americans. But Congress later abandoned those efforts. As a result, African Americans still did not have rights that other Americans enjoyed.

In the twentieth century, African Americans continued the work left undone by Reconstruction. They used peaceful methods to challenge segregation and policies that kept them from voting. They filed lawsuits in courts and they carried out nonviolent protests. By the 1960s, African Americans had made great progress toward ending segregation and gaining voting rights. It had taken a century, but many of the goals of Reconstruction had finally been realized.

An African-American man protests unequal treatment at Woolworth's in the 1960s. This is one example of many protests waged during the civil rights movement, which gained equal rights for African Americans.

TIMELINE

1854 Congress passes the Kansas-Nebraska Act. This law allows residents in those territories to decide whether to permit slavery.

Americans opposed to the Kansas-Nebraska Act form the Republican Party.

1860 Abraham Lincoln is elected president of the United States.

On December 20, South Carolina secedes from the Union.

1861 On April 12, Southern forces fire on Fort Sumter in Charleston Harbor, South Carolina. The Civil War begins.

1863 President Lincoln issues the Emancipation Proclamation on January 1.

On December 8, Lincoln announces his Ten Percent Plan for restoring Southern states to the Union.

1865 On April 9, Confederate general Robert E. Lee surrenders to Union general Ulysses S. Grant. The Civil War ends.

John Wilkes Booth assassinates President Lincoln on April 14. Andrew Johnson becomes president.

On May 29, Johnson outlines his plan for Reconstruction. Radical Republicans in Congress believe the plan is too lenient.

The Thirteenth Amendment is ratified on December 6.

1867 On May 2, Congress passes the Reconstruction Act of 1867. This law sets up military rule in most of the South.

1868 On February 24, the House of Representatives votes to impeach Johnson. By May, the U.S. Senate does not have enough votes to remove Johnson from office.

The Fourteenth Amendment is ratified on July 28.

1870 The Fifteenth Amendment is ratified in March.

1877 Federal troops end the occupation of Louisiana and South Carolina. Reconstruction ends.

American Moments

FAST FACTS

In January 1865, General William T. Sherman issued Special Field Order No. 15. This order set aside land in South Carolina and Georgia for freed slaves. Eventually, about 40,000 former slaves settled on the land. After the Civil War, this land was taken away from them.

Many soldiers lost arms and legs in the Civil War. A year after the war, the state of Mississippi set aside one-fifth of its budget to buy artificial arms and legs for veterans.

The Freedmen's Bureau built about 1,000 schools for African Americans and helped about 200,000 slaves learn how to read. After the Civil War, African Americans also raised money to build schools. Many skilled African-American workers donated their talents to construct school buildings.

During Reconstruction, Pickney Benton Stewart Pinchback served as the first African-American governor. He was governor of Louisiana from December 1872 to January 1873. Pinchback filled the governor's position while the previous governor was involved in an impeachment proceeding.

For more than 100 years, Andrew Johnson had been the only president to be impeached. But in 1998, the House of Representatives voted to impeach President William J. Clinton. The Senate tried Clinton on charges of lying under oath and obstruction of justice. Clinton was not found guilty of the charges.

WEB SITES
WWW.ABDOPUB.COM

Would you like to learn more about Reconstruction? Please visit **www.abdopub.com** to find up-to-date Web site links about Reconstruction and other American moments. These links are routinely monitored and updated to provide the most current information available.

Lady Liberty leads the Union army in bringing freedom to the slaves. On the right, Lincoln holds the Emancipation Proclamation.

GLOSSARY

amnesty: an act by the government that forgives someone of an illegal deed.

apprenticeship: the condition of an apprentice. An apprentice learns a trade or craft from a skilled worker.

arsenal: a collection of weapons, or a place where weapons are made.

Confederate States of America: the country formed by the states of South Carolina, Georgia, Florida, Alabama, Louisiana, Mississippi, Texas, Virginia, Tennessee, Arkansas, and North Carolina that left the Union between 1860 and 1861. It is also called the Confederacy.

Constitutional Union Party: a political party formed on May 9, 1860. The party wanted to find a peaceful solution to the slavery issue. After the 1860 election, the party broke apart because of the Civil War.

Democractic: a political party. During the Civil War, it supported farmers and landowners.

discrimination: treating a group of people unfairly based on characteristics such as race, class, or gender.

emancipation: the act of freeing someone from slavery.

impeach: to charge a government official with wrongdoing in office.

Quaker: a member of the religious group called the Society of Friends.

Republican: a political party. During the Civil War, Republicans were liberal and against slavery.

secede: to break away from a group.

sentinel: a soldier standing guard.

servitude: the condition of serving a master, slavery.

telegraph: a system of communication made of wires in which messages are transmitted electronically.

vagrancy: wandering around without employment or a home. Vagrancy is often considered a crime.

veto: the right of one member of a decision-making group to stop an action by the group. In the U.S. government, the president can veto bills passed by Congress. But Congress can override the president's veto with a two-thirds majority vote.

Whig: a political party that was very strong in the early 1800s, but ended in the 1850s. Whigs supported laws that helped business.

INDEX